CHINA

Compiled and Edited by

TONY CURTIS

First Published   July   1976
Reprinted   Dec.   1976
"   April   1977
"   Aug.   1977
Revised Edition   June   1978

Exchange Rate $2 = £1

Original Edition   ISBN 902921-43-6
Revised Edition   ISBN 902921-66-5

Copyright © Lyle Publications 1977.
Published by Lyle Publications, Glenmayne, Galashiels, Scotland.
Distributed in the U.S.A. by Apollo, 391 South Road, Poughkeepsie, N.Y. 1260

INTRODUCTION

Congratulations! You now have in your hands an extremely valuable book It is one of a series specially devised to aid the busy professional dealer in his everyday trading. It will also prove to be of great value to all collectors and those with goods to sell, for it is crammed with illustrations, brief descriptions and valuations of hundreds of antiques.

Every effort has been made to ensure that each specialised volume contains the widest possible variety of goods in its particular category though the greatest emphasis is placed on the middle bracket of trade goods rather than on those once - in - a - lifetime museum pieces whose values are of academic rather than practical interest to the vast majority of dealers and collectors.

This policy has been followed as a direct consequence of requests from dealers who sensibly realise that, no matter how comprehensive their knowledge, there is always a need for reliable, up-to-date reference works for identification and valuation purposes.

When using your Antiques and their Values to assess the worth of goods, please bear in mind that it would be impossible to place upon any item a precise value which would hold good under all circumstances. No antique has an exactly calculable value; its price is always the result of a compromise reached between buyer and seller, and questions of condition, local demand and the business acumen of the parties involved in a sale are all factors which affect the assessment of an object's 'worth' in terms of hard cash.

In the final analysis, however, such factors cancel out when large numbers of sales are taken into account by an experienced valuer, and it is possible to arrive at a surprisingly accurate assessment of current values of antiques; an assessment which may be taken confidently to be a fair indication of the worth of an object and which provides a reliable basis for negotiation.

Throughout this book, objects are grouped under category headings and, to expedite reference, they progress in price order within their own categories. Where the description states 'one of a pair' the value given is that for the pair sold as such.

Printed by Apollo Press, Dominion Way, Worthing, Sussex, England.
Bound by Newdigate Press, Vincent Lane, Dorking, Surrey, England.

CONTENTS

A mid 19th century Ashworth's Ironstone dinner service of fifty pieces. $670 £335

ATTIC POTTERY

An attic pottery owl skyphos, 5th century B.C. $360 £180

A black figure band cup decorated with syrens between figures, Athens, 530 B.C. $1,080 £540

An attic black figure kylisi, 16¾ins. diam., 540-530B.C. $4,950 £2,475

BEERSTEINS

A large pottery beerstein painted in blue and brown with relief designs of armed classical figures and other designs, 12ins. high. $48 £24

An impressive three litre Imperial German pottery beerstein. $110 £55

A fine, old Imperial German half-litre painted pottery beerstein, 11¼ins. high. $130 £65

A small 19th century Belleek jardiniere.
$80 £40

Belleek porcelain jardiniere with birds and flowers in high relief, 20ins. high.
$120 £60

A Belleek lattice work basket. $150 £75

Rare Belleek figure of a tinker woman, her clothes sparsely tinted with yellow.
$270 £135

Pair of Belleek candelabra. $310 £155

Belleek hot water vessel and stand. $310 £155

Belleek centrepiece, 12¾ins. high. $360 £180

Belleek spill vase, the fluted cornucopia with a bronzed putto kneeling at the foot. $520 £260

Elaborate double-spouted kettle by Belleek, the spouts in copper lustre, on a dragon stand. $1,000 £500

9

BERLIN

19th century Berlin porcelain plaque. $80 £40

A Berlin porcelain oval plaque of a young nun, set in a gilt frame, 9ins. high. $120 £60

19th century Berlin cup and saucer. $240 £120

A good Berlin plaque painted in subdued colours and showing a young girl in a long flowing dress, signed 'Wagner', impressed 'K.P.M.', 8½ins x 5¾ins. $300 £150

19th century K.P.M. porcelain vase and cover. $350 £175

Berlin rectangular plaque painted with the 'Beggar Boys' after Murillo, 7¾ ins. wide. $430 £215

One of a pair of fine Berlin vases. $500 £250

German porcelain plaque painted with a female saint playing the organ, 12½ins. wide. $670 £335

One of a pair of ormolu mounted Berlin porcelain vases, circa 1890, 41in. high. $44,000 £22,000

10

Blue grandmother Reynolds'

19th century Bow
seated putto. $120 £60

Blue and white Bow
mug, circa 1760.
$180 £90

One of a pair of 18th
century quail-pattern
Bow octagonal plates,
4ins. diam. $230 £115

Bow jug decorated with
a Kakiemon design, 5ins.
high, circa 1765. $300 £150

A fine Bow
shepherdess.
$350 £175

Early Bow sauceboat,
the squat body with
shaped rim, circa 1752,
9in wide. $460 £230

An early Bow porce-
lain figure of a
parrot. $1,250 £625

Bow figure of the
'Indiscreet Harlequin',
circa 1750, 7ins. high.
$1,490 £745

One of a pair of Bow
figures of Kitty Clive
as the Fine Lady, and
Henry Woodward as
the fine Gentleman in
Garricks farce 'Lethe'.
$3,080 £1,540

11

BRUSSELS FAIENCE

An early Brussels faience tureen depicting a hen with chicks.
$1,500 £750

A very rare Brussels faience tureen in the form of a duck.
$2,750 £1,375

A rare Brussels faience tortoise tureen.
$3,750 £1,875

CAPO-DI-MONTE

A rare Royal Vienna style fairing with the Naples Capo Di Monte mark.
$480 £240

Capo Di Monte figure of Pantaloon from the Italian comedy, modelled by Guiseppe Gricci, 15cm. high.
$7,700 £3,850

'The Declaration', by Giuseppe Gricci.
$26,400 £13,200

Rare Capodimonte figure by Giuseppe Gricci, circa 1745.
$32,000 £16,000

Capo Di Monte figure of a sempstress by G. Gricci.
$44,000 £22,000

Extremely rare Capodimonte Commedia Dell'Arte group of the Harlequin and two other figures by Giuseppe Gricci dated around 1750.
$64,000 £32,000

Small fan-shaped
asparagus server in
Caughley porcelain,
circa 1780-90.
$50 £25

Caughley porcelain egg-
drainer and 'waster',
circa 1780-90. $60 £30

Early 19th century
Caughley pickle dish
$60 £30

Caughley cream jug in
underglaze blue, circa
1780, 3¼ ins. high.
$64 £32

A Caughley pear-
shaped coffee pot,
with floral decor-
ation, 8ins. high,
with 'C' mark.
$96 £48

Caughley miniature
tea bowl and saucer,
'Fisherman Pattern'.
$100 £50

19th century Caughley
jug. $120 £60

18th century Caughley
fluted teapot, cover
and stand, decorated
in blue and gilt. $120 £60

Rare Caughley
hyacinth pot,
8in. high, about
1780-85 $760 £380

13

Rare Red Anchor period Chelsea chocolate cup, cover and saucer, boldly painted in polychrome with fruits, circa 1755. $180 £90

Chelsea yellow tiger plate of octagonal form. $360 £180

Chelsea beaker, Kakiemon, red anchor. $380 £190

One of a pair of Chelsea botanical plates. $740 £370

A pair of Chelsea figures of a youth and maiden carrying baskets, 7ins. high, gold anchor mark. $840 £420

A 19th century pottery figure of 'The Piccadilly Rose Woman', by Vyse Pottery, Chelsea. $1,100 £550

Chelsea teapot and cover by Jeffryes Hamett O'Neale, 6½ins. high. $1,260 £630

Set of Chelsea figures of the elements with gold anchor marks, 9ins. high. $1,450 £725

Chelsea botanical plate, one of a pair. $1,680 £840

Chelsea Hans Sloane meat dish, red anchor. $1,730 £865

A red anchor period Chelsea dovecot, 17 ins. high. $2,000 £1,000

Chelsea triangle period acanthus leaf moulded cream jug, circa 1746. $2,040 £1,020

Chelsea beaker decorated with acanthus, triangle mark. $2,110 £1,055

Chelsea triangle 'Goat and Bee' jug, circa 1745, 3¾ins. high. $2,160 £1,080

A strawberry dish in Chelsea porcelain, 3¾ins. diam. $2,280 £1,140

One of a pair of Chelsea bottles, modelled on a Japanese original, decorated in the Kakiemon style, 7¼ins. high. $2,970 £1,485

Pair of Chelsea bird models with feathers decorated in coloured enamel and the beak, heads and feet similarly treated, 4¾ins. high. $4,650 £2,325

Chelsea cream jug, triangle mark. $5,280 £2,640

15

CHELSEA

Very rare Chelsea coloured acanthus leaf cream jug, 3½ ins. high, of the triangle period with crown and trident mark. $5,500 £2,750

Chelsea Red Anchor botanical plate of the Hans Sloane type, with a red anchor mark.
$6,800 £3,400

One of a pair of Chelsea artichoke tureens, 5ins. diam. $12,760 £6,380

Chelsea porcelain teapot and cover, 17.8cm. wide.
$13,400 £6,700

A pair of Chelsea porcelain parakeets, 5ins. high.
$14,320 £7,160

Chelsea figure of a Chinese man, 7ins. high. $17,600 £8,800

Chelsea tureen, in the form of a pair of billing doves, 17ins. wide. $20,900 £10,450

Chelsea teapot in the shape of a Chinese man and parrot, 7ins. high. $34,000 £17,000

Boar's head tureen, in Chelsea porcelain, the stand, 22ins. long. $70,400 £35,200

CHELSEA DERBY

CHELSEA DERBY

A 19th century Chelsea Derby vase, with patch marks and incised numerals, 11ins. high. $150 £75

Chelsea Derby figure of a young man, patch marks, 5½ins. high.
$190 £95

Chelsea Derby jug decorated with green and gilt floral swags, circa 1770, 4¾ins. high. $310 £155

COALBROOKDALE

Modern Coalbrookdale urn. $300 £150

A large 19th century Coalbrookdale centre-piece, 18ins. high.
$350 £175

Coalbrookdale vase decorated with panels showing peasants on one side and gentle-folk on the other. 20½ins. high $860 £430

Coalbrookdale flower-encrusted vase.
$1,010 £505

A fine Coalbrookdale plate with four matching engraved wine glasses 1855. $1,250 £625

Coalbrookdale plate from a service which Queen Victoria presented to the Tsar of Russia in 1845, 9¾ins. diam. $1,800 £900

17

A red and gilt
Coalport cup
and saucer. $24 £12

Coalport teapot, circa
1840-45.　　$90 £45

Early Coalport spill
vase.　　$100 £50

l9th century Coalport
vase.　　$100 £50

Henrietta, circa 1750,
china figure by Coalport,
7ins. high.　$230 £115

Coalport jug printed
in dark blue, 21.5cm.,
high.　　$260 £130

Part of a Coalport tea service of thirty-seven pieces with mark
number 946, circa 1825.　　　　　　　$600 £300

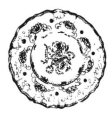

One of a set of twelve
Coalport plates. $650 £325

19th century English porcelain
garniture of three vases in the
Sevres manner, probably
Coalport. $700 £350

Coalport vase and cover
with a panel of fruit
framed by gilt rococo
scrolling, 12ins. high,
1900. $860 £430

Rare lustre lamp and cover,
probably Coalport, circa
1800, 9½ins. high. $1,630 £815

One of a pair of Coalport
rose-pompadour vases and
covers, by William Cook,
1861, 14½ins. high.
$2,970 £1,485

One of a pair of Coalport
rose-pompadour vases and
covers, 1861, 15½ins. high.
          $3,200 £1,600

A Coalport plate from a
set of 24, signed by P.
Simpson, 9ins.
          $3,200 £1,600

Large Celeste blue Coalport
vase with panels by James
Rousse, 30¾ins. high,
1861. $4,300 £2,150

19

COMMEMORATIVE CHINA

A china commemorative cream jug, Coronation of H.M. King Edward VII.
$10 £5

Pottery jug with black Jackfield type glaze, 1897.
$12 £6

Edward VIII Coronation cup.
$12 £6

Porcelain Peace mug of the first world war, 1918.
$12 £6

1937 Coronation mug.
$12 £6

Porcelain George and Mary Coronation beaker, 1911, 4ins. high.
$14 £7

Earthenware mug showing Lord Roberts of the Boer War. $20 £10

Cream earthenware mug to commemorate the coronation of Edward VIII.
$40 £20

Earthenware mug with portrait of present Queen as a child.
$50 £25

Earthenware mug with transfer of a cricketer, dated 1924-5. $50 £25

A jug depicting The Prince of Wales mounted on a pony and inscribed 'England's Future King'. $70 £35

Mug to commemorate the marriage of the Duke of York and Princess May. $80 £40

Mug to celebrate the opening of Miller Park, Preston. $90 £45

A Victorian jug produced for the marriage in 1840. $90 £45

A mug produced for the christening of the Prince of Wales on January 10th, 1842. $170 £85

Rare commemorative puzzle jug, sides painted in pink lustre, circa 1816, 7ins. high. $480 £240

Rare Victorian Proclamation mug printed in pink. $480 £240

Earthenware coronation mug of Queen Victoria. $1,320 £660

Copeland Spode teapot. $20 £10

Blue and white transfer printed small oval dish, impressed Copeland, and No. 6, circa 1850, 8½ins. long. $20 £10

Copeland and Garrett jug, circa 1845. $40 £20

Copeland pineapple jelly mould, circa 1860. $44 £22

19th century Copeland cigar box with a fish and netting decoration, 7in. high. $70 £35

An attractive white and gilt Copeland spoon warmer in the form of a large sea shell, on seaweed and coral base, circa 1850, 4½ins. high. $70 £35

Copeland and Garrett tureen, cover and stand, circa 1860. $70 £35

One of a pair of Copeland two-handled vases with floral spray and gilt decoration. $80 £40

Large Copeland tazza printed in orange and green with brown and black overprinting. $140 £70

DAVENPORT

DAVENPORT

Octagonal Davenport Longport porcelain dessert plate, circa 1870. $24 £12

Davenport cup and saucer. $24 £12

Marked Davenport plate, 10ins. diam. $40 £20

An early 19th century Davenport stone china dinner service of 103 pieces. $1,000 £500

DELFT TILES

Late 18th century Dutch ship tile. $16 £8

Late 17th century Dutch tile. $30 £15

Mid 17th century Dutch Cavalier tile. $30 £15

18th century Delft
plate painted with
flowers in under-
glaze blue, 23cm diam.
$16 £8

One of a pair of
Victorian Delft
vases. $48 £24

An unusual small
18th century Delft
hand. $60 £30

A Delft, blue and
white oval plaque,
well painted with a
street scene, inscribed
in Dutch below, 20 ins
wide. $104 £52

18th century blue and
white Delft drug
jar, 'V. Galeni', 7½ ins
high. $140 £70

An early 18th century
Bristol Delft ware
polychrome plate.
$180 £90

London Delft wet drug
jar, first half of 18th
century, 8 ins high.
$310 £155

One of a pair of
18th century Delft
drug jars.$360 £180

Delft 'Adam and Eve'
charger, (damaged).
$600 £300

One of a set of four blue and white Dutch Delft Season plates, 8¾ ins diam. $700 £350

An early Dutch Delft pottery cow. $700 £350

Delftware polychrome dish decorated in blue, iron-red and green, circa 1710. $710 £355

One of a pair of 18th century English Delftware wet drug jars. $720 £360

17th-18th century London Delft Barber's bowl, 10 ins diam. $770 £385

Bristol Delft vase decorated with two lion masks and landscapes, 11 ins high. $1,000 £500

Lambeth Delft cup, dated 1715 and initials I.H.F. $1,080 £540

17th century Dutch Delft tulip vase and cover, 23 ins high. $1,200 £600

London Delft 'Sack' bottle inscribed in blue, 5ins. high, 1651. $1,200 £600

A rare London Delft plate commemorating John Wilkes's controversial 45th issue of 'The North Briton', in 1763. $1,250 £625

An English Delft inkwell, decorated with scattered flower-sprays. $1,460 £730

English Delft blue dash charger depicting General Monck, circa 1665. $1,980 £990

18th century English Delft blue and white Barber's bowl. $2,640 £1,320

Bristol Delft punch bowl. $3,500 £1,750

An English Delft charger depicting Adam and Eve, 16¼ins. diam. $3,750 £1,875

A good blue and white Southwark Delft mug. $3,850 £1,925

17th century Delft posset pot, decorated in blue with an inscription and date, 1651. $4,620 £2,310

Dutch Delft tureen, cover and stand, marked in blue G.V.S., circa 1765. $23,100 £11,550

Unmarked Derby dish with
handles, circa 1820. $40 £20

A Derby putto circa
1770-1775. $60 £30

Derby inkstand with
standard painted
mark in red circa
1800. $100 £50

Large 19th century
urn-shaped Derby vase
14 ins high. $100 £50

Early 19th century
Derby figure. $150 £75

A 12 ins shaped Crown
Derby dish 'Near
Sydersham', circa
1800-1825. $150 £75

Victorian Derby
candlestick. $150 £75

Derby teapot decorated
with a traditional Imari
pattern. $180 £90

One of a pair of Derby
style figures support-
ing candle holds.
$230 £115

27

Modern Royal Crown Derby peacock. $380 £190

Large and rare Derby tankard painted with a sportsman and his dog, 5¼ins. tall. $420 £210

Derby female figure, circa 1770, 13ins. tall. $430 £215

Derby 'Admiral Rodney' jug, 9¼ins. high. $480 £240

One of a pair of Derby candlestick figures, about 1770. $900 £450

Crown Derby teapot painted in polychrome enamels, 4½ins. high, factory mark in blue. $1,010 £505

Part of a Derby dessert service painted with fruit, nuts, flower sprays and insects. $9,200 £4,600

Shaped Dresden bowl with cover having gilt, yellow and floral garland decorations with figure panels. $30 £15

19th century Dresden plate. $30 £15

19th century Dresden porcelain mirror decorated with flowers and surmounted with cupids. $60 £30

19th century Dresden comport. $60 £30

A pair of 19th century white Dresden figures, 8ins. high, of a young man and a young girl. $72 £36

A plate from a 19th century Dresden part dinner service decorated in blue and white, with twenty-two plates, oval ashet and a sauce boat. $200 £100

19th century Dresden group, 6ins high. $260 £130

Part of a set of John Gilbert fruit knives and forks with Dresden handles in porcelain, about 1870. $380 £190

Pair of Dresden figures of Malabur musicians playing a lute and hurdy-gurdy, 12 ins high. $480 £240

our Dresden Lamp 28" Sotheby

Pale BLUE "pierced"

19th century Dresden pierced and flower encrusted comport, 17½ins. high. $500 £250

Part of a 24-piece 19th century Dresden dinner service. $550 £275

Large Dresden ewer moulded in high relief with mermaids, seahorses and Neptune. $550 £275

One of a pair of Dresden candelabra with the crossed swords mark, 9½ins. high. $620 £310

19th century Dresden figures depicting 'Spring, Summer, Autumn and Winter'. $620 £310

One of a pair of Dresden vases 21 ins high, circa 1860. $950 £475

Potschappel (Dresden) circular punch bowl, having a knop modelled as two children. $1,600 £800

A large Dresden vase and cover, 25 ins high, with a pair of vases and covers painted and encrusted with flowers, 16¾ ins high. $1,870 £935

One of a pair of Dresden lemon ground vases and covers, 24½ ins high. $2,420 £1,210

Royal Doulton art pot about 1902-22, 7½ ins high x 8½ ins deep. $30 £15

One of a pair of Doulton ware spill vases with flowers and panels of fish in bas-relief, 10¼ins. high. $40 £20

Doulton (Lambeth) art pot, 8½ins. high x 10ins. deep. $84 £42

Doulton stoneware tea set decorated by Hannah Barlow and dated 1875. $180 £90

Doulton water set by Hannah Barlow 1885. $220 £110

A pair of Doulton stoneware vases decorated by Hannah Barlow. $350 £175

A Doulton stoneware vase by Arthyr Barlow, dated l875. $820 £410

31

Royal Doulton floral toilet jug. $20 £10

Royal Doulton green and white toilet jug and basin. $36 £18

Royal Doulton jardiniere with blue, fawn and floral decoration. $36 £18

One of a pair of Royal Doulton vases having blue brown and green decoration, 7 ins tall. $36 £18

Royal Doulton bone china figure of 'Fragraise', 5½ ins high. $36 £18

Large Royal Doulton vase with blue, green and flower decoration. $60 £30

A tall Royal Doulton vase in deep blue and smeared light green stoneware. $72 £36

A pair of Royal Doulton pattern 8814 relief moulded floral design vases, signed E.B., 12½ ins high. $84 £42

A Royal Doulton pattern relief moulded lily pattern jardiniere signed M.B., 9ins. high. $84 £42

Doulton Lambeth salt-glaze jug. $24 £12

Stoneware ale barrel tap, impressed "Doulton & Co., Lambeth, London", circa 1869. $44 £22

A 10in. high Doulton Lambeth jug with raised decoration. $44 £22

Doulton Lambeth Victoria Jubilee jug, 7 ins high. $52 £26

Doulton Lambeth silicone vase with white and fawn decoration in relief, 9½ins. tall. $60 £30

Doulton Lambeth urn with raised stag and foliage decoration, 16 ins high. $120 £60

Circular Doulton Lambeth salad bowl having blue and fawn decorations with plated rim and matching plated servers. $120 £60

Small pair of Doulton Lambeth vases, dated 1880 and monogrammed by Florence Barlow. $300 £150

Pair of Doulton Lambeth vases by Florence Barlow. $340 £170

One of a pair of
Exeter pottery vases.
$18 £9

English porcelain jug
and two tumblers,
circa 1880. $20 £10

Allerton toby jug,
1912. $24 £12

Rodgers pottery sauce-
boat with underglaze
blue rim, circa 1790.
$24 £12

English blue and
white pottery plate
circa, 1770. $30 £15

An Adams tray with a
black slip ground and
applied white classical
figures, 9 ins. x 12 ins.
$34 £17

Isnik dish by Frank
Brancywyn. $36 £18

Early 20th century
St Cecilia studio pottery
vase. $40 £20

Blue transfer pottery
shaped oval dish,
possibly Turner, circa
1780, 12¼ ins long.
$46 £23

A rare blue and white transfer printed ashet decorated with acrobats, marked Middlesbrough. $64 £32

Early 19th century Chemist's honey jar with gilt lettering on Royal Blue band, 10½ins. high, circa 1820. $66 £33

Thomas Hanley pottery teapot, circa 1805.
$90 £45

Admiral John Jellicoe jug by Carruthers Gould. $90 £45

Early 19th century Pinxton bowl on a waisted foot, 6½ins. diam. $180 £90

Silver resist jug of large size, 6½ ins. high, circa 1810.
$230 £115

Pottery teapot dated 3l March 1786 and marked with a C.
$230 £115

18th century strapwork basket the centre depicting exotic birds and flower sprays, 6½ ins diam.
$260 £130

Decorated pottery dish by H.Schiltt. $290 £145

ENGLISH

Wafer-thin Queensware dish decorated in puce, about 1725. $300 £150

An early English leaf dish. $340 £170

Caneware jug about 1795. $480 £240

Yorkshire pottery cow-creamer. $530 £265

Pair of Victorian figures depicting street traders, 9in. high. $960 £480

A Nantgarw plate with bird decoration. $960 £480

Beaker from the Giles workshop. $960 £480

A very rare Bristol flower holder of cruciform shape. $1,080 £540

One of a pair of Burdett Coutts' plates. $1,390 £695

A rare cream jug, with figure of 'Long Eliza' picked out in coloured enamels, 3¼ ins high. $1,800 £900

Rare slipware teapot decorated in 'Sgraffiato' technique. $2,160 £1,080

Early 19th century serving dish with gilt decoration on salmon pink ground, enclosing a coat of arms, 19½ins. long. $2,040 £1,020

A rare commemorative Bragget pot of large size, possibly by Ralph Simpson, circa 1700, 7¼ ins high. $2,750 £1,375

A superb pair of two-handled vases by Harry Davis. $3,080 £1,540

One of a pair of cream-ware figures of Hamlet and Ophelia, glazed in green and brown. $3,520 £1,760

Heart shaped pill slab painted with the Arms of Charles II, 9½ ins long. $6,160 £3,080

English porcelain figure of a seated hound, by the 'The Girl-in-a-Swing' factory, circa 1750, 10.8 cm high. $7,920 £3,960

Slipware dish, probably by William Taylor. $7,920 £3,960

FRENCH

One of a pair of 19th century French pottery plates, decorated with portrait medallions, 8ins. diam. $60 £30

One of a pair of mid 19th century French porcelain figures.
$96 £48

19th century French bisque porcelain bust named Du Barry, with pale polychrome colours. $116 £58

Pair of octagonal based Limoges candlesticks, 6¼ins. high. $530 £265

Chantilly two handled bowl, 11ins. wide.
$530 £265

Pair of Jacob Petit vases circa 1860. $580 £290

18th century French glazed teapot.
$720 £360

One of a fine pair of French vases and covers, 11 ins high.
$1,020 £510

One of a pair of 19th century Felspar vases with ormolu rams head handles and mounts, 30 ins high.
$1,500 £750

One of a pair of French faience jardinieres from Nevers. $2,890 £1,445

A fine Marseilles faience plate, with fish and lobster design.
$2,400 £1,200

One of a pair of 19th century French oviform vases with royal blue and gilt lids and ormolu mounts, 35¼ ins. high. $2,900 £1,450

Chantilly figure of a Chinese man, 7ins. high.
$3,700 £1,850

A Marseilles faience two-handled tureen and cover painted in colours with bouquets of flowers, 36cm wide. $4,620 £2,310

Sceaux faience duck tureen, 12ins. long.
$6,600 £3,300

One of a pair of Vincenne cabbage leaf tureens with covers and stands.
$6,930 £3,465

One of a fine pair of ormolu mounted Mennecy figures.
$22,000 £11,000

Mid 16th century French pottery ewer, decorated with stamped and inlaid designs, 34 cm high.
$96,800 £48,400

GERMAN

German bisque musician figure vase. $30 £15

German matchholder of a kitten in porcelain, with a fluted green basket on either side, circa 1890.
$30 £15

A small 19th century German porcelain figure of a gentleman holding his hat. $34 £17

Interesting old Imperial German porcelain desk ornament by Rosenthal, Bavaria, 7½ ins high.
$110 £55

Pair of 19th century German china pin boxes entitled Grandmama and Grandpapa.
$144 £72

A Cologne ovoid vase.
$144 £72

19th century German porcelain rhinoeerus 13 ins long in naturalistic colours with a cream underbelly. $180 £90

Finely modelled 19th century German pottery pug in natural colours of grey and cream, 18½ ins long. $200 £100

One of a pair of German porcelain figures of dogs, 12 ins long. $230 £115

40

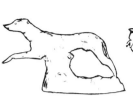

One of a pair of
porcelain greyhounds 12 ins
long, Hochst 1790.
$480 £240

One of a pair
of Sitzendorf
candelabra,
19½ins. high.
$480 £240

One of a pair of 19th
century German vases
decorated with country
scenes. $550 £275

A pair of Frankenthal figures of Harvesters,
4 ins high. $960 £480

Porcelain ice-bucket from
the Nymphenburg factory,
6½ ins high. $1,200 £600

Well executed plaque from the Mettlach
factory in Germany depicting Greek
soldiers in white relief on a grey green
ground. $1,250 £625

A fine pair of elaborately
decorated Potschappel
china jars, 31 ins high.
$1,920 £960

19th century Goss crested jug, 3¾ ins high. $10 £5

Bideford mortar, by Goss. $12 £6

Goss swan, 4.7in. long. $60 £30

Goss penguin, 88mm. long. $160 £80

Goss wall pocket of a cherub $170 £85

Goss model of Campbelton Cross, 145mm. high. $180 £90

Goss mask of a knight. $320 £160

Porcelain lithophane disc, 3½in. diam., by Goss. $600 £300

Fine Goss figure of William of Wykeham on circular base, 8in. high. $1,400 £700

Goss model of
Shakespeare's
Cottage. $60 £30

Shakespeare's House,
78mm. long. $70 £35

A Goss Cottage, 'A
Window in Thrums'.
$120 £60

The large night-light
version of Shakespeare's
House by Goss. $120 £60

'St Nicholas Chapel,
Ilfracombe, by Goss.
$120 £60

A Goss model of The
Tudor House,
Southampton.
$290 £145

Goss Old Thatched
Cottage, Poole. $290 £145

A Goss model of the
Old Market House,
Ledbury. $360 £180

A rare Goss piece, Isaac
Walton's Cottage,
Shallowford. $480 £240

43

ITALIAN

One of a pair of large Italian St. Denis grey-ware vases decorated with figures of girls and landscapes in panels, 21ins. high. $210 £105

A south Italian red figure Amphora 350-325 BC, 16 ins high. $530 £265

Shallow dish painted with a bust of Caesar, dated 1540 by Castel Durante. $1,250 £625

A large Deruta jar, early 16th century, 34cm. high. $2,400 £1,200

A good Le Nove figure group. $2,400 £1,200

Florentine medicine jar painted in colours, circa 1480, 23.5cm high. $8,800 £4,400

Late 15th century Faenza alberello painted in colours with a portrait of a girl. $14,500 £7,250

A majolica plate, the central reserve showing a satyrical Peeping Tom watching two ladies having a bathe in a lagoon, 11¾ins. diam. $59,000 £29,500

A blue and white bowl in Medici porcelain, made in the late 16th century, 5 ins diam. $150,000 £75,000

19th century gilt and floral decorated earthenware jardiniere and pedestal. $200 £100

Victorian hand painted jardiniere stand with an unusual vase shaped pot. $220 £110

Victorian floral decorated jardiniere and stand. $250 £125

A Bretby earthenware jardiniere with turquoise blue glazed medallions. $280 £140

An Art Nouveau jardiniere and stand by Bretby featuring imitation jewels and a shipping scene. $300 £150

Victorian jardiniere and stand, circa 1890. $400 £200

Mid 19th century simulated green marble jardiniere and stand. $440 £220

One of a pair of French style jardinieres and stands, circa 1870, decorated in brown, yellow and green. $650 £325

45

LAMBETH

A Lambeth standing salt, 4ins. high.
$1,060 £530

English Lambeth bowl painted in blue and initialled R. A. M., circa 1718. $5,940 £2,970

Lambeth drinking cup of tin glazed pottery in blue on a manganese ground, 10cm high, 1635. $10,400 £5,200

LEEDS

Leeds underglaze blue plate. $48 £24

18th century Leeds pottery teapot and teaware. $310 £155

One of a pair of silver resist vases, probably Leeds, circa 1810, 6½ ins high.
$360 £180

Leeds creamware seated sphinx, circa 1770. $440 £220

A rare pair of Leeds pink lustre figures of a 'Shepherd' and 'Shepherdess', circa 1810, 7¾ ins high. $720 £360

18th century Leeds creamware mug.
$900 £450

Blue and white
Liverpool Coffee
Pot, circa 1785.
$140 £70

Liverpool jug in under-
glaze blue by Seth
Pennington, circa 1785.
$200 £100

Liverpool mug
painted in
famille rose
colours.
$400 £200

Large Liverpool
Chaffer's Jug
decorated with
a chinoiserie
landscape, 9½ins.
high. $480 £240

Liverpool bowl
by William Ball,
circa 1760.
$1,010 £505

Pair of Liverpool
vases by William
Reid, 11 ins
high, circa 1775.
$1,870 £935

LONGTON HALL

Longton Hall coffee
cup, circa 1758-60.
$110 £55

Longton Hall jug decorated
with bouquets of flowers,
8ins. high. $1,440 £720

A superb Longton
Hall melon tureen,
4.7/8ins wide.
$8,800 £4,400

Lowestoft jug with
kick-back handle and
pink border, 3¼ins.
high, circa 1785.
$120 £60

Charming Oriental
teapot from the
Lowestoft factory,
about 1775.
$440 £220

Lowestoft blue and
white octagonal ink-
well, circa 1762-65.
$580 £290

Lowestoft blue
and white mug,
circa 1757-60.
$620 £310

Lowestoft pap warmer,
10¼ins. high, circa
1765. $840 £420

Lowestoft porcelain
teapot, inscribed
and dated.
$1,340 £670

Lowestoft blue and
white mug, circa
1765-68. $1,340 £670

Commemorative Lowestoft
mug of cylindrical form,
circa 1775, 4½ ins high,
restored. $1,490 £745

Lowestoft blue and
white coffee pot,
circa 1757-60.
$3,010 £1,505

A copper lustre
jug, with figures
in relief, 7½ ins
high. $30 £15

Victorian plaque
inscribed 'Prepare
to Meet Thy God'.
$34 £17

Lustre mug in
underglaze
blue with brick
red flower
design, circa
1830, 3 ins
high. $36 £18

Victorian lustre jug.
$40 £20

Welsh lustre jug with
blue ivy pattern on
side with raised
stags under a tree,
circa 1835, 6½ ins
high. $68 £34

Copper lustre jug
with raised ribbed
border, 4ins. high.
$68 £34

Gilded pottery jug
with silver lustre
and red decoration,
circa 1810. $84 £42

Victorian lustre
punch bowl.
$100 £50

Rare jug of ovoid form,
with pink lustre neck,
probably Sunderland,
about 1815. $640 £320

Early 19th century silver lustre pottery figures of Apollo and Diana, 10½ ins high. $340 £170

One of a pair of early 19th century vases of compana shape, probably Leeds, decorated on a pink lustre ground, 6¼ ins high. $860 £430

Early 19th century lion passant, covered overall in mottled pink lustre, 12 ins long. $1,680 £840

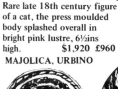

Rare late 18th century figure of a cat, the press moulded body splashed overall in bright pink lustre, 6½ins high. $1,920 £960

A rare Sunderland pink lustre set of the seasons, impressed Dixon, Austin and Co., circa 1820, 9 ins high. $2,420 £1,210

MAJOLICA, URBINO

17th century Italian majolica dish depicting the Rape of the Sabines. $1,640 £870

Rare Urbino Istoriato dish of Cardinal's hat form, 26cm. diam. $6,270 £3,135

A superb Urbino dish by Franceso Xanto Avelli da Rovigo, depicting the story of Actaeon and his encounter with Diana 17 ins. diam. $50,000 £25,000

Martinware potiche, signed and dated 1907, decorated with fish and jelly fish in a yellow green sea, 2½ ins high. $84 £42

Martinware vase, circa 1902. $96 £48

Martin Brothers stoneware pitcher. $110 £55

A Martinware tobacco jar and cover in the form of a bird, circa 1906. $780 £395

Pair of Martinware lovebirds. $840 £420

Late 19th century Martinware bird with a bored and super-cilious look, 8¾ ins high, ice-grey/blue in colour. $1,100 £550

Late 19th century Martinware bird doing its best to look like a penguin. $1,460 £730

Late 19th century Martinware 'Monk' bird. $1,750 £875

One of a set of three Martinware figures of a pottery thrower, with the impressed mark R.W. Martin, dated 1884, 7¼ ins high. $2,860 £1,430

MASON'S

19th century ironstone export platter, 1847. $24 £12

A Mason's ironstone china circular soup tureen and cover. $36 £18

Mason's ironstone serving dish, circa 1813. $48 £24

19th century Mason's ironstone blue and white toilet jug and basin. $48 £24

Mason's ironstone tureen, circa 1830. $160 £80

An ironstone vase and cover with pineapple finial, (A.F.), 37ins. high. $260 £130

A pair of Mason's ironstone covered vases, with Korean lion handles and Chinese style decoration, 15¼ins. $290 £145

Part of a sixty-one piece Mason's ironstone 'Japan' pattern dinner service. $720 £360

52

Early 19th century Meissen teapot. $144 £72

Mid 19th century Meissen male and female figure with cross swords mark in underglaze blue. $190 £95

Early 19th century Meissen tureen, 43cm. wide. $200 £100

Meissen hen on a nest. $230 £115

One of a pair of Meissen figures each supported by a conch shell posy vase. $360 £180

Meissen Kakiemon dish, 4½ins. square. $360 £180

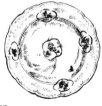

Meissen figure of a swan. $430 £215

A pair of 19th century Meissen porcelain pot pourri vases with pierced domed covers, painted with flowers and birds, 14¼ ins high. $440 £220

Meissen plate with cross swords mark, circa 1750. $540 £270

MEISSEN

Meissen octagonal lilac ground cup and saucer. $570 £285

19th century Meissen figure group, 15 ins high. $770 £385

One of a pair of Meissen figures, circa 1840, 1ft 11 ins high.
$960 £480

Late Meissen group of Count Bruhl's tailor after the smaller model of 1737.   Mid-19th century. $960 £480

One of a pair of 19th century Meissen groups.
$1,030 £515

A good beaker in Meissen porcelain.
$1,310 £655

Meissen ecuelle cover and stand decorated with a mixture of chinoiserie and European subjects.
$1,510 £755

A pair of Meissen goldfinches.
$1,620 £810

One of a pair of Meissen brocaded Imari plates.
$1,800 £900

One of a pair of
Meissen figures
of Harlequin and
Columbine by
Kandler. $2,000 £1,000

A fine Meissen
ecuelle, cover
and stand.
$2,400 £1,200

An early Meissen
porcelain milk jug
and cover with
its original silver
gilt mounts, by
Elias Adam of
Augsburg. $2,400 £1,200

Meissen porcelain
parasol handle.
$2,640 £1,320

Tureen from late
Meissen onion
pattern service.
£2,640 £1,320

A Meissen teapot
and cover, 6¼ ins
high. $3,230 £1,615

A pair of Meissen pagoda
figures by J.J. Kandler,
7¼ ins high. $3,190 £1,595

An early Meissen Hausmaler
Goldchinesen milk jug and
cover by Bartholmaus
Seuter, 18.5cm.
$3,410 £1,705

'The Spanish Lovers'
by Johann Joachim
Kandler, 1741,
17.8cms. $5,080 £2,540

55

One of a pair of Meissen cock and hen teapots and covers modelled by J.J. Kandler, 21.5cm wide. $6,000 £3,000

Meissen thimble, decorated in Schwarzlot and gold by Ignaz Preissler, 2.4cm high. $9,070 £4,535

A fine Meissen teapot decorated at Augsburg, 4½ins. high. $9,900 £4,950

An early Meissen porcelain yellow ground vase, 13½ in. high. $19,800 £9,900

Lady and blackamoor in Meissen porcelain, by J.J. Kandler, 7½ ins. long. $22,000 £11,000

Figure of a Bustard by Johann Joachim Kandler, Meissen, circa 1732, 84cm high. $28,000 £14,000

German Meissen porcelain snuffbox decorated to commemorate the First Silesian War by Johann Jacob Wagner, with English gold mount. $33,490 £16,745

Early Meissen figure of a Pagod in a pavilion, circa 1715, 6¾ ins. $57,200 £28,600

Meissen coffee pot by Sabina Aufenwerth of Augsburg, circa 1731, 21.3cm high. $88,000 £44,000

Victorian Minton tile. $12 £6

Minton comport with green ground and floral decoration. $12 £6

19th century circular Minton plate with blue, gilt and flower decorations. $14 £7

Minton art pot, dating between 1895-1900 in a single shade of green mint, 8½ins. high x 10in. deep. $56 £28

Minton figure of a child taking off shoes, 3½in. high, circa 1840. $84 £42

Oval embossed Minton game tureen with holly leaf decoration and cover surmounted by a hunting dog with gun and bag, circa 1873. $120 £60

Minton parian figure of Solitude by J. Lawbor, circa 1852. $130 £65

19th century Jasper ware Stilton dish from the Minton factory, 12ins. long, 12ins. high. $160 £80

19th century Minton jardiniere and stand coloured purple with an attractive white wash effect. $200 £100

Minton earthenware figure of a Sea Horse with Shell, 14in. high, richly decorated with majolica glazes, about 1855. $200 £100

Minton earthenware figure of a man with a wheelbarrow draped with hop branches, about 1870, 13½ins. high. $240 £120

Minton earthenware figure of a monkey holding fruit, about 1860. $360 £180

Minton figure of a Guitar Player and Harper, circa 1835. $540 £270

A pair of Minton vases painted by W. Mossill, 15ins. high. 1876. $620 £310

One of pair of Minton vases decorated with pictorial cupid scenes, on ormolu bases, 16ins. tall. $780 £390

One Minton pate-sur-pate vase with cover, 15½in. tall. $1,860 £930

Part of a Minton dessert service comprising twenty-two plates and five tazzas. $1,150 £575

An important early Minton vase, 28ins. high. $2,040 £1,020

MOORCROFT

MOORCROFT

Moorcroft pottery vase painted with fruit and foliage on a dark blue ground, circa 1930. $72 £36

Pair of Moorcroft pottery mallet shaped vases painted with chrysanthemums, circa 1920. $120 £60

William Moorcroft teapot 1898, painted with blue poppies. $150 £75

MORGAN

19th century De Morgan tile. $50 £25

A De Morgan vase of copper lustre decoration, on a cream ground, from the late Fulham period, 1898-1907, 15¾ ins. high. $790 £395

Late 19th century Wm. de Morgan lustre dish depicting a reindeer beneath an orange tree. $860 £430

A William de Morgan dish of Persian influence, of the late Fulham period. $860 £430

A De Morgan vase of Persian influence, with deep blue ground, of early Fulham period, 15ins. high. $1,100 £550

Late 19th century De Morgan earthenware vase painted by Fred Passenger and depicting stylised Hispano-Moresque cranes. $1,870 £935

A small Victorian earthenware vase, inscribed "Never too late to mend" $4 £2

A sugar bowl from the Dartmouth pottery, bearing the legend, 'Waste not, want not' $4 £2

A Dartmouth pottery jug, inscribed 'No road is long with Good Company'. $4 £2

An unmarked pottery hot-water jug. $8 £4

An Aller Vale pottery hat-pin stand, decorated with ship design. $8 £4

An unmarked earthenware coffee-pot, the motto cut through the white slip to the brown clay. $8 £4

An Aller Vale pottery teapot bearing the legend, 'Ye may get better cheer, But no' wi' better heart'. $8 £4

A Barnstaple pottery jug. $10 £5

A tile from the Watcombe pottery, decorated with leaf and flower swirls. $16 £8

Newhall lustre cup
and saucer with
bird's nest design,
circa 1815. $36 £18

Silver shaped teapot of
the Newhall factory is
marked with the number
195, dating it to 1787-90.
$140 £70

Rare Newhall water jug
with hand-painted coat
of arms and landscape,
circa 1810. $170 £85

PARIAN

Victorian white
moulded parian jug
with foliate decor-
ation, circa 1861.
$24 £12

Victorian parian
female figure 12 ins.
$60 £30

19th century parian
figure of a nude
reclining on the
back of a lion. $120 £60

Minton parian figure
of Colin Minton Campbell,
about 1875, 19in. hight.
$190 £95

Parian bust of Queen
Victoria, signed Noble,
2ft. high. $500 £250

Jug showing the
famous brass
quintet of the
Distin father and
sons, in parian ware,
about 1850, 14in.
high. $720 £360

PARIS

An attractive Paris porcelain plinth, finely painted with a woodland scene, 10ins. diam. $66 £33

Pair of Paris figures, 8 ins high. $100 £50

An early 19th century Paris porcelain vase of powder blue ground with gold scroll decoration and a polychrome panel $200 £100

One of a pair of Paris vases with rich gilt necks, feet and scroll handles, 18¾ins high. $310 £155

Pair of Paris porcelain vases decorated with country scenes, 21in. high. $480 £240

A 19th century Paris vase by Francois Boucher. $720 £360

PLYMOUTH

Pair of Plymouth figures of boy military bandsmen, 11ins. and 10½ins. high. $720 £360

An unusual Plymouth bell-shaped tankard, decorated with a group of Chinese musicians, 6¼ins high. $2,270 £1,135

Pair of Plymouth figures depicting a gardener and his companion, 1768-1771. $2,640 £1,320

Poole pottery vase by
Truda Carter, circa
1927, 8 ins high.
$30 £15

Poole pottery unglazed
jug, 8 ins high, 1930.
$50 £25

Poole pottery two-
handled vase, circa 1924.
$50 £25

Poole pottery green
glazed vase with
sculptured handles
in white, circa 1925.
$100 £50

Poole pottery fish
glazed in green
with a black base,
17 ins high. $120 £60

Poole pottery vase with
impressed mark, Carter
Stabler Adams Ltd.,
England, 18 ins
high, 1927. $130 £65

PRATTWARE

Prattware plate 'The Hop
Queen' with charact-
eristic malachite
pattern border. $100 £50

19th century Prattware
teapot and stand.
$200 £100

One of a rare pair of
Prattware vases.
$1,680 £840

ROCKINGHAM

Small 19th century Rockingham dish with cover. $50 £25

An early 19th century Cadogan teapot made by Rockingham.
$110 £55

A Rockingham cup, with the distinctive griffin mark in red and painted with a bouquet of flowers. $580 £290

A fine and rare Rockingham cat, seated upon a cushion. $620 £310

A Rockingham shepherdess, 6¾ ins high. $680 £340

Rockingham style twenty seven piece botanical dessert service comprising eighteen 9 ins diameter plates and nine comports of shell, oval and square shapes. $960 £480

English Rockingham porcelain tankard painted with a portrait of the Duke of Wellington, circa 1830.
$1,920 £960

Rockingham plate from a service made for William IV 9½ ins diam.
$2,350 £1,175

Rare Rockingham figure of John Liston as 'Billy Lackaday', circa 1826, 6 ins high.
$4,400 £2,200

ROYAL DUX

ROYAL DUX

19th century Royal Dux group of a child playing with a dog. $130 £65

Pair of Royal Dux figures in classical dress, 16 ins. high.
$150 £75

19th century Royal Dux figure of a seated girl with a shell. $150 £75

RUSKIN

A Ruskin cylindrical shaped vase with orange lustre glaze, 25cm high. $68 £34

Ruskin flared cylindrical vase with yellow lustre glaze 30.5cm high.
$48 £24

A Ruskin shouldered pottery vase circa 1905.
$84 £42

Ruskin pottery vase.
$100 £50

Ruskin pottery vase circa 1906. $110 £55

Ruskin eggshell pottery bowl, circa 1910.
$130 £65

RUSSIAN

Lilac and grey transfer printed plate with centre view of St Petersburg, circa 1865, 10 ins diam. $44 £22

A Kornileffe Bros. ink stand pentray decorated with polychrome floral sprigs and gilding. $170 £85

A fine Paul I, St. Petersburg verriere. $360 £180

A Russian figure of a dancer, circa 1830. $400 £200

A good Nicholas II porcelain urn decorated with figures. $720 £360

Dessert set of 16 pieces of St Petersburg porcelain, 1777. $9,200 £4,600

SAMPSON

A Sampson china circular jardiniere, the blue ground with gilt decoration and reserves of Chinese scenes, 9in. diam. $48 £24

19th century Sampson of Paris figure. $120 £60

A Sampson imitation of a Bow figure of Harlequin and Columbine. $260 £130

An amusing saltglaze fish gin flask with impressed scales and fins, cork in opened mouth, 12in. long, circa 1820. $90 £45

19th century saltglaze puzzle jug. $96 £48

Heavily saltglazed stoneware ale pitcher, the handle formed from a greyhound, 10in. high, circa 1830. $120 £60

Saltglaze pottery Toby jug of Lord Nelson, 10½ ins high. $120 £60

One of a pair of saltglaze stoneware tobacco jars named 'Flake' and 'Mixture' 10 ins high. $170 £85

Saltglazed stoneware spirit flask of Old Tom, by Oldfield and Company. $180 £90

London saltglaze stoneware commemorative tankard of cylindrical shape, dated 1741, probably Fulham, 8½ ins high. $360 £180

Octagonal saltglaze plate. $560 £280

Saltglaze bear jug and cover, with outstretched paws, being attacked by a dog, 9¾ins high, circa 1740. $620 £310

SALTGLAZE

Amusing saltglaze camel teapot, about 1750.
$960 £480

One of a pair of saltglaze cups, the lower half moulded with gadroons, circa 1760, 3ins. high. $1,100 £550

Saltglaze ermine spot teapot.
$1,440 £720

Saltglaze punch pot and cover painted with Bacchus.
$1,680 £840

Turquoise ground saltglaze cream jug. $1,730 £865

Saltglaze plate with the monogram T.H., 9ins. diam.
$2,280 £1,140

A fine saltglaze polychrome punch pot.
$3,000 £1,500

English saltglaze figure of a piper, about 1740-45, 19cm high.
$4,400 £2,200

Important saltglaze group of lovers.
$10,000 £5,000

68

Sevres ice cup decorated with Angouleme springs. $80 £40

Sevres pierced oval fruit dish, circa 1810. $120 £60

A late 19th century Sevres inkstand. $120 £60

A 19th century Sevres group 'The Lovers with Cupid'. 9ins. high, 8½ins. long. $120 £60

Pair of Sevres pattern vases and covers, 11½ins. high. $230 £115

One of a pair of Louis Phillipe Sevres portrait plates, the centre decorated with portraits of Louis XV and Luxinka. $240 £120

Early 19th century Sevres tazza mounted on an ormulo base. $420 £210

Pair of Sevres covered vases of compressed pear shape, 7¾in. high, 1754. $530 £265

One of a pair of Sevres jardinieres decorated with a continuous band of figures in a garden, having ormolu mounts, 8¾in. high. $530 £265

Sevres pattern cabaret set painted with lovers in landscapes. $530 £265

An early 18th century Sevres porcelain plaque.
$580 £290

Pair of Sevres pattern turquoise ground vases and covers, 13ins. high.
$600 £300

Sevres globe with cupids and ormolu handles.
$600 £300

One of a pair of good quality 19th century Sevres vases decorated with a coastland scene.
$600 £300

One of a set of eight Sevres plates painted with Royal portraits of Louis XVI and Marie Antoinette.
$720 £360

Sevres pattern cabaret set richly decorated on a blue ground, in a fitted leather case.
$1,080 £540

70

A Sevres casket modelled as an open fan, 33cm wide. $1,150 £575

One of a pair of Sevres porcelain and ormolu wall sconces. $1,300 £650

Sevres-pattern yellow-ground ormolu-mounted bowl with red printed mark, circa 1850, 20in. wide. $1,440 £720

One of a fine pair of 19th century Sevres vases decorated with figures and landscapes on a deep blue ground, 2ft. 6ins. high. $2,100 £1,050

An early Sevres porcelain and ormolu jardiniere.
        $2,200 £1,100

One of an important pair of Sevres vases of urn shape with gilt ormolu mask head handles, 25¼ins. high, 1764.
        $2,260 £1,130

Sevres vase, porcelain.
    $2,860 £1,430

Pair of Sevres pattern ormolu mounted vases painted with the Birth of Jesus and the Triumph of Ariadne, 34ins. high. $3,400 £1,700

One of a pair of early 19th century Sevres vases. $4,300 £2,150

SEVRES

One of a pair of 19th century French china and ormolu mounted vases in the Sevres style, 33½ins. high.
$4,290 £2,145

Sevres ewer and basin painted by Jean Dubois, 1757. $4,950 £2,475

An important Sevres porcelain vase in the Louis XVI manner signed C. Labarre, 3ft. 4ins. high.
$4,950 £2,475

Sevres blue lapis divided jardiniere, 1758, 10¾ins. wide. $6,000 £3,000

Pair of Sevres-pattern vases decorated with Napoleonic scenes by Despres, 55½ins. high.
$15,400 £7,700

One of an extremely fine pair of Sevres 'Rose Pompadour' vases. $19,800 £9,900

Part of a French Sevres porcelain dinner service of 145 pieces, circa 1775.
$28,000 £14,000

A fine Louis XV table with a Sevres porcelain plaque forming the top surrounded by a pierced brass gallery.
$28,050 £14,025

Circular two-handled tureen, cover and stand from the Sevres ornithological service.
$74,000 £37,000

Spode, blue and
white egg stand.
$20 £10

19th century Spode
milk jug. $24 £12

'Tiber' plate with
pierced edge,
marked Spode.
$50 £25

'Gothic Castle'
vegetable tureen,
marked Spode. $60 £30

An 8½in. hexagonal
Spode plate with bird
and feather decoration,
circa 1790-1820. $72 £36

A marked Spode comport
'Long Eliza'. $96 £48

'Tower' two-handled
covered centre bowl,
marked Spode. $100 £50

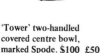

A very rare marked Spode
'Forest Landscape' dog's
dish. $110 £55

Rare Spode oviform
vase, 7in. high,
early 19th century.
$420 £210

STAFFORDSHIRE ANIMALS

A fine early 19th century Rockingham retriever. $60 £30

19th century Staffordshire dalmatian. $50 £25

Staffordshire sheep, circa 1840. $30 £15

An early Staffordshire cow creamer decorated in tan and sepia, on an octagonal green base, 8ins. long. $76 £38

A Staffordshire vase group of a cow and calf, circa 1855, 11ins. high. $84 £42

A Staffordshire zebra on base of green rocks, circa 1845, 9ins. high. $96 £48

19th century Staffordshire hen on nest.$110 £55

A pair of Staffordshire King Charles spaniels, coloured black and white with gilt collars, 12½in. high, circa 1850. $116 £58

One of a pair of large Staffordshire pug dogs circa 1870. $120 £60

74

mine have a "free foot" making them more valuable.

Late Victorian figure of Jumbo (started life London Zoo 1865, died charging a train in Ontario 1885). $120 £60

An amusing pair of rough chip coated poodles in Staffordshire pottery, circa 1850, 10½ins. high. $140 £70

A very rare Staffordshire flat back orange cow, originally used as a dairy shop sign, circa 1845, 13ins. high, 13½ins.long. $160 £80

Staffordshire monkey musician playing cello, Toby jug, circa 1845. $200 £100

A rare pair of Staffordshire pugs, white with black markings, circa 1865, 10½in. high. $200 £100

Staffordshire pottery cow-creamer, 6¼ins. $340 £170

Rare figure of the champion greyhound Master McGrath. $410 £205

Rare Staffordshire 'Jumbo'. $420 £210

'The Roran Lion' by Obediah Sherratt. $600 £300

STAFFORDSHIRE

Staffordshire soup
bowl, circa 1825.
$10 £5

Staffordshire willow
pattern cup and
saucer, circa 1860.
$12 £6

Small Victorian
Staffordshire
bowl and vase.
$30 £15

19th century
Staffordshire
brown clay jug
8½ ins. high.
$30 £15

Very large cup and saucer
in Flo blue underglaze
pottery, decorated with
a figure on a bridge, Royal
Staffordshire Pottery,
Burslem, circa 1885.
$64 £32

Early 18th century
Staffordshire stags
head cup. $66 £33

A very rare Staffordshire
Toby jug in the form of a
King Charles spaniel, with
blue scroll handle, circa
1850, 8in. high. $80 £40

19th century Stafford-
shire pottery jug
showing two hunting
scenes, 6½ins. high.
$96 £48

One of pair of Staffordshire
children's plates bearing a
portrait of Queen Victoria.
$170 £85

An unusual coloured Staffordshire Toby jug, named 'Merry Christmas', 7in. high, circa 1845. $180 £90

Old Staffordshire slip decorated cradle of yellow on a brown ground. $180 £90

A tobacco jar, with a tavern scene, in 19th century Staffordshire. $240 £120

Staffordshire jug with portraits of William IV and Queen Adelaide, 6 ins. high, puce printed. $240 £120

One of a pair of Staffordshire magenta ground earthenware leech jars, 28ins. high, circa 1835. $900 £450

Rectangular table snuff box, South Staffordshire about 1770. $1,080 £540

Early Staffordshire dish dated 1773. $1,260 £630

Vase decorated with Chinese figures, probably made in Staffordshire. $2,750 £1,375

A tulip girl Staffordshire slipware dish, by Ralph Toft, 16¾ins. diam. $16,500 £8,250

STAFFORDSHIRE FIGURES

19th century group of a young man and woman. $36 £18

Staffordshire group of a seated boy and girl with dog, 14ins. high. $36 £18

Staffordshire dancing figure of a sailor's lass, circa 1850. $44 £22

19th century, Staffordshire figure of Byron, 7ins. tall. $60 £30

Staffordshire figure of Mrs. Glover and Mrs. Vining, circa 1840. $72 £36

19th century Staffordshire figure of the Duke of Edinburgh. $72 £36

19th century figure of 'Girl and Gallant' on a scroll end settee, 8ins. long. $84 £42

Hollow based Staffordshire sailor, circa 1830. $84 £42

Staffordshire figure 'Going to Market'. $84 £42

Staffordshire Sampson-Smith figure named 'Queen of England'. $90 £45

Staffordshire figure of Marnaud, circa 1854. $110 £55

Staffordshire figure of a 'Fortune Teller', 12ins. high. $110 £55

Early Staffordshire figure of a 'Showman' by Ralph Salt, circa 1820. $110 £55

Square based Staffordshire figure of Peace burning the helmet of Mars, 8½ins. high. $120 £60

Stafford group of Hamlet, Shakespeare and Lady Macbeth, circa 1848. $120 £60

Figure of 'Sanky', an American evangelist, 12½ins. high. $144 £72

Staffordshire figure of 'The Widow', 11ins. high. $144 £72

A fine unrecorded Staffordshire figure of Milton, resting on a pedestal and holding a book, 9in. high. $160 £80

STAFFORDSHIRE FIGURES

Staffordshire portrait figure of Queen Victoria and Princess Royal.
$160 £80

Pair of figures of Uncle Tom and Eva, 8ins. high.
$170 £85

A rare Staffordshire group of three figures, named 'Turkey, England & France', depicting Abdul-Medjid, Queen Victoria and Napoleon III, circa 1854, 11¼ins. high. $190 £95

Pair of figures depicting Victoria and Albert, 11½ins. high. $220 £110

Staffordshire figure of a lion tamer with three lions and a leopard. 15cm high. $290 £145

Pair of figures depicting Uncle Tom and Aunt Chloe, 8¾ins. high.
$360 £180

Equestrian figure of Marshal Arnaud.
$480 £240

An important pair of Staffordshire bust figures of William IV and Queen Adelaide.
$500 £250

'Othello and Iago'.
$580 £290

Figure, possibly representing
Mlle. Alboni as Cinderella,
sitting in a pumpkin coach
drawn by a prancing horse.
$840 £420

Equestrian figure of
Abdul-Medjid, Sultan
of Turkey, 11in. high.
$600 £300

Figure of Jenny Lind
as Alice in Meyerbeers
opera, 13¾ins. high.
$620 £310

Staffordshire figure
'The Grapplers'.
$1,740 £870

Fine Staffordshire figure
'The Vicar and Moses',
9½ins. high. $840 £420

Pair of early 19th century
Staffordshire figures of
Tom Cribb and Molineaux,
21.5cm high. $1,730 £865

Rare Staffordshire
equestrian figure of
Sir Robert Peel.
$3,700 £1,850

English Staffordshire
figure of a piper,
circa 1730, 23.5cm
high. $7,480 £3,740

King William III English
Staffordshire pottery,
circa 1770-75, 39.3cm
high. $12,760 £6,380

81

Staffordshire model of 'Stansfield Hall'. $70 £35

Staffordshire model of a 'Gothic Castle'. $96 £48

A rare Staffordshire pottery castle, named 'Sebastopol', circa 1855. $110 £55

Staffordshire porcelain pastille burner cottage, circa 1840. $120 £60

Attractive porcelain cottage with Gothic windows. $120 £60

Victorian Staffordshire pastille burner. $130 £65

Porcelain toll-house with lift off roof. $144 £72

White porcelain castle with green grass, leaves and colourful flowers. $300 £150

Porcelain castle rich with roses and other flowers. $300 £150

19th century stoneware quart jug. $44 £22

Old stoneware tobacco jar with bas-relief Royal coat of arms with lion and unicorn supporters, circa 1830, 7½ins. high. $60 £30

Salt glazed stoneware flask of the Duke of York. $190 £95

SUNDERLAND

Sunderland lustre plate, 'Thou God Seest Me'. $48 £24

A Sunderland ware bowl, with transfer printed panels of the Cast Iron Bridge over the River Wear, 12½ins. diam. $84 £42

A Sunderland ware jug, with transfer printed panels, 8½ins. high. $84 £42

SWANSEA

An attractive black transfer Swansea pottery plate, circa 1820, 8¾ins. diam. $60 £30

Rare Victorian Swansea coronation mug printed in purple. $360 £180

Part of a rare Swansea cabaret, comprising a coffee pot and cover, milk jug, slop bowl, teacup and saucer and tray. $2,400 £1,200

Victorian feeding cup. $8 £4

Victorian chamber pot. $10 £5

Victorian stone hot water bottle. $10 £5

Pair of Victorian pottery figures 6ins. tall. $16 £8

Blue and white china cheese dish and cover, circa 1890. $16 £8

Victorian milk jug with a pewter lid. $18 £9

Late 19th century decorated vase. $18 £9

Pair of Victorian china bookends in the form of children. $18 £9

Victorian moustache cup and saucer. $20 £10

A Victorian biscuit barrel with a plated lid. $20 £10

Fine Victorian moustache cup with floral decoration.
            $20 £10

Victorian decorated pot pourri vase and cover. $20 £10

Victorian green ground two handled vase with floral decoration. $20 £10

Victorian jug and basin. $20 £10

Victorian pottery vase with applied decoration.
            $20 £10

Earthenware nine position pig foster mother. $28 £14

Victorian floral toilet pail with a wicker handle. $30 £15

Victorian decorated china fruit bowl.
            $34 £17

Victorian pottery
footbath. $36 £18

19th century
Fishley toad
plate. $40 £20

Large Victorian
decorated bowl.
$40 £20

One of a pair of
Victorian vases,
14ins. high. $50 £25

A white ware double
toilet set of nine
pieces, with hand
painted Lily of the
Valley flowers. $60 £30

Large Victorian
jardiniere. $60 £30

Large late 19th
century blue and
white cheese dish.
$64 £32

Flamboyant green,
yellow, gold and
white teapot, dates
to within three years
of 1843, made by
Samuel Alcock. $70 £35

An unusual pottery
cheese dish and cover,
with white orange skin
body and polychrome
raised Japanese stylised
flowers, 9ins. high.
$90 £45

Florian vase made at MacIntyres, circa 1893. $100 £50

One of a pair of Victorian 'Mama and Papa' figures, circa 1895. $110 £55

A two-handled urn with shell decoration, 14ins. high. $110 £55

Late 19th century jardiniere, 14½ins. high $110 £55

A large 19th century circular jardiniere decorated with a landscape, 29ins. high. $144 £72

Victorian unglazed decorated figurine of a musician and flower girl. $160 £80

19th century vase with a cut out dolphin motif on a salmon pink ground. $190 £95

One of a pair of Brownfield's Geisha flower vases, 11ins., printed with date code for October 1899. $230 £115

Rare moulded plaque of the young Victoria. $240 £120

VIENNA

Vienna urn shaped tureen decorated with blue and red roses, tulips and forget-me-nots. $210 £105

Vienna tea-for-two service. $400 £200

One of pair of Viennese china baluster vases richly decorated with classical figures. $1,390 £695

Vienna porcelain plaque depicting Columbus' return from his voyage to the New World, 16ins. diam. $1,080 £540

One of a superb pair of Vienna vases, 21ins. high. $3,740 £1,870

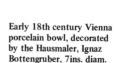

Vienna rectangular dish with fish shaped handles decorated in monochrome enriched with gold, circa 1730. $5,500 £2,750

A rare teapot by Vezzi of Venice, circa 1720 (damaged spout). $6,400 £3,200

Early 18th century Vienna porcelain bowl, decorated by the Hausmaler, Ignaz Bottengruber, 7ins. diam. $13,200 £6,600

19th century green Wedgwood serving plate. $16 £8

Wedgwood stepped conical vase with grey glaze signed Keith Murray, 18cm. high $16 £8

A marked Wedgwood ashet, 8ins. long.$28 £14

19th century impressed upper case Wedgwood botanical plate, 9¼ins. diam. $30 £15

Pair of late 19th century Wedgwood candlesticks 5ins. tall. $48 £24

19th century Wedgwood pagoda pattern, shaped dish, 10ins. long. $48 £24

Wedgwood 8in. plate in polychrome enamels, circa 1820. $76 £38

19th century Wedgwood blue and white teapot. $84 £42

19th century blue and white Wedgwood biscuit barrel with silver mounts. $110 £55

One of a pair of 18th century Wedgwood green ground vases, 8ins. tall. $150 £75

Unusual bamboo teapot made by Wedgwood in 1871. $220 £110

Early 19th century black basalt female figure, 11ins. high. $320 £160

Black basalt 'Etruscan' vase, probably Wedgwood and Bentley, circa 1770, 10¼ins. high. $360 £180

Wedgwood creamware teapot and cover, decorated probably by David Rhodes, 8½ins., impressed mark. $360 £180

19th century Wedgwood vase and stand. $410 £205

Wedgwood green and white, jasper plaque, depicting classical figures. $410 £205

A Wedgwood black basalt bust of Lord Byron, 15ins. high. $480 £240

Jasper dip Wedgwood vase, about 1860, 25.5cms. high. $500 £250

18th century
Wedgwood pot
pourri jar.
$540 £270

A fine Wedgwood
Wheildon tortoise-
shell glazed teapot.
$550 £275

One of a pair of Wedgwood
earthenware plaques by
S. Bateman, 1886.
$670 £335

A rare Wedgwood
caneware bulb
trough, 14½in.
long. $740 £370

One of a pair of 19th
century Wedgwood
white stoneware, covered
urns, mounted with gir-
dles of dancing women.
$770 £385

Wedgwood Queens
Ware tureen
decorated with
overglaze decoration,
circa 1790.
$840 £420

Small 18th century
Wedgwood three
colour vase. $840 £420

A pair of Wedgwood
black basalt busts,
9¼in. high. $860 £430

Victorian Wedgwood
circular plaque painted
by Emile Lessore.
$910 £455

An unusual Wedgwood punch bowl, the interior painted in black and sepia enamels with various masonic emblems.
$1,150 £575

A good Wedgwood and Bentley variegated creamware urn shaped vase. $1,200 £600

Wedgwood and Bentley blue jasper plaque with half-length figures of Pan and faun, about 1775.
$1,250 £625

Paid $45.00 in 1985.

Empress Josephine 1804-1809 my plaque

The Wedgwood 'Pegasus' vase.
$2,040 £1,020

Pair of Wedgwood variegated creamware vases and covers, circa 1780, 21cm. high.
$2,040 £1,020

Wedgwood and Bentley urn and cover, circa 1775, 37.5cm. high.
$3,300 £1,650

Blue and white jasper ware plaque of 'The Three Graces', circa 1775, with the mark of Wedgwood and Bentley, 28.6cm. wide. $3,960 £1,980

Wedgwood and Bentley basalt pottery wine ewer. $12,000 £6,000

Copy of the Portland vase by Josiah Wedgwood, circa 1790. $40,000 £20,000

A very fine example of
a Wheildon pottery plate,
with raised spotted shaped
border, circa 1760. $116 £58

Very rare Whieldon
tea caddy and cover,
6¾in. high, 1760-
65. $1,040 £520

One of a very fine
pair of Wheildon
glazed pottery
squirrels.
       $5,940 £2,970

WOOD

Enoch Wood mustard
pot, circa 1835.
           $60 £30

Late 18th century bust
of Minerva. $380 £190

Fine bust of Napoleon
by Enoch Wood.
           $400 £200

A fine Ralph Wood, Jnr.,
tree trunk vase with a
figure at the base.
           $660 £330

Rare Ralph Wood Toby
jug, circa 1750, translucent
glaze, tortoiseshell coat,
blue hair and breeches and
a restored hat. $660 £330

A Ralph Wood
St. George and
Dragon. $960 £480

Royal Worcester white leaf design pot. $40 £20

Royal Worcester fish decorated plate 10½ ins diam., circa 1870. $48 £24

Royal Worcester jug with floral decoration and a gilt handle, 4¾ ins tall, circa 1891. $84 £42

Royal Worcester cream and gilt decorated two handled pot with cover. $84 £42

A Royal Worcester china circular bowl with gilt double handles, 10¼ ins diam. $180 £90

Royal Worcester porcelain figure of 'The Bather Surprised', with gilt decoration. $290 £145

A Royal Worcester china ewer shaped vase of the Victorian period, 16ins high. $300 £150

Pair of 19th century Royal Worcester female figures. $410 £205

Royal Worcester jardiniere. $410 £205

An extremely fine,
intricately decorated
and encrusted Royal
Worcester vase,
19 ins high. $540 £270

Pair of 19th century Royal
Worcester figures.
$540 £270

A pot pourri vase and
cover painted by
James Stinton, date
symbol 1908, 7 ins
high. $600 £300

One of a pair of Royal
Worcester vases of
Persian form, painted
and signed T.J. Bott,
circa 1877. $720 £360

Pair of late 19th century Royal
Worcester male and female
Japanese figures, 16 ins high,
dated 1871 and 1875 $800 £400

A Royal Worcester
vase and cover, the
body painted by
John Stinton,
signed, 16½ ins
high, 1898.
$1,640 £820

Vase and cover by
John Stinton with
highland cattle scene
in a mountainous
landscape, 1914,
19½ ins high.
$2,210 £1,105

A pair of Royal Worcester
vases painted by Harry
Davis, bearing the date
mark for 1911.
$3,080 £1,540

One of a pair of red
cardinals in Royal
Worcester porce-
lain, modelled by
Dorothy Doughty,
10 ins high.
$3,460 £1,730

CHAMBERLAIN WORCESTER

One of a pair of Chamberlain's Worcester vases, 6½ins. high. $84 £42

A Chamberlain's Worcester bottle vase and cover of double wall construction, 9¾ins. high. $120 £60

Chamberlain Worcester, meat platter, family crest in centre, 16½ins overall length, circa 1810. $200 £100

Part of a Chamberlain's Worcester dessert service with apple green borders and centres, painted with botanical flowers, comprising three shaped dishes, and three plates. $370 £185

Part of a set of four Chamberlain's Worcester plates and two dishes, 9¼ ins diam. $420 £210

A Chamberlain's Worcester plate painted with peacocks and exotic birds. $460 £230

Rare set of five Chamberlain Worcester figures of the Rainer brothers and their sisters, 6ins. high, complete with an original signed lithograph. $3,850 £1,925

Flight, Barr and Barr cup and saucer, impressed and under-glazed printed marks. $110 £55

A Flight, Barr and Barr, Worcester vase of apple green ground with floral paintings on each side. $180 £90

Worcester teapot, marked Flight, Barr and Barr, 1807-13. $260 £130

A Worcester Flight, Barr and Barr dessert service decorated in rouge de fer, red, blue and gilt with gadrooned border, comprising two small tureens and covers, one large comport, three oval dishes, four square dishes, three shell dishes and twenty-one side plates. $820 £410

Worcester Barr part dessert service. $1,730 £865

Flight, Barr and Barr feather painted part tea and coffee service, late 18th/ early 19th century. $1,800 £900

WORCESTER

Worcester cup and saucer, circa 1840.
$24 £12

Worcester porcelain shell dish on three ball feet, 9ins. long, circa 1895. $60 £30

A 19th century Worcester blue and white pickle dish. $80 £40

A first period Worcester blue and white plate.
$120 £60

One of a pair of Grainger sauce tureens, circa 1810.
$160 £80

Unusual Worcester chocolate ground cup and saucer.
$180 £90

Worcester teapot, about 1751-83, in printed porcelain.
$210 £105

One of a set of ten Worcester dessert plates, each finely painted by E. Salter.
$230 £115

First period Worcester, interlaced strapwork basket, 6½ins. diam.
$360 £180

A Crescent Worcester chocolate pot.
$380 £190

A first period Worcester cup and saucer, decorated with flowers and butterflies.
$380 £190

Worcester blue ground loving cup with fruit decoration. $460 £230

First period Dr. Wall porcelain sucrier with lid, with floral decoration. $460 £230

A blue and white Worcester pot pourri bowl. $480 £240

One of a pair of Worcester porcelain dishes. $480 £240

First period Worcester 'Chelsea ewer' shaped jug with rococo handle, 3½ins. high, circa 1762.
$580 £290

Worcester blue and white tureen and cover, circa 1758.
$580 £290

A first period Worcester tankard, depicting an Oriental scene. $600 £300

First period
Worcester
teapot. $780 £390

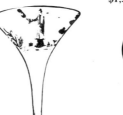

A fine first period Worcester
blue and white bottle vase
with knopped and flared
trumpet neck, 11ins. high.
$670 £335

First period
Worcester
coffee pot.
$1,010 £505

Worcester sucrier and
cover with flower knop,
circa 1770, 4½ins. high.
$1,050 £525

Worcester blue and white
vase, 22ins. high, circa
1753. $1,440 £720

Dr. Wall Worcester
blue scale jug.
$1,560 £780

Worcester blue and
white bowl depicting
an Oriental scene,
circa 1758. $1,800 £900

Early Worcester
porcelain wine
funnel, 4½ins.
high. $2,420 £1,210

One of a pair of small
Dr. Wall apple green
vases, 5¾ins. high.
$2,750 £1,375

A fine Dr. Wall period
hot water jug complete
with cover. $3,080 £1,540

A superb early
Worcester
sauceboat. $3,080 £1,540

A fine and rare Worcester
porcelain vase and cover
by James Hadley, 1888,
23½ins. high. $4,290 £2,145

A very fine Worcester
butter tub, cover and
stand, painted in the
'Earl Manvers' pattern,
circa 1770.
$7,040 £3,520

One of a pair of early
Worcester figures of
a Turk and his female
companion, 5ins. high.
(slight damage)
$7,150 £3,575

An exceptionally fine
early Worcester group
of two birds.
$7,150 $3,575

A superb first period
Worcester tankard,
6ins. high.
$7,700 £3,850

English Worcester
porcelain bowl of the
Dr. Wall period with
three painted panels
on a turquoise ground,
circa 1770.
$21,000 £10,500

An early Worcester
porcelain cream boat,
2½ins. high.
$44,000 £22,000

WROTHAM

Red pottery with white slip Tyg by Thomas Ifield of Wrotham, Kent, 13.3cm high, 1652. $2,420 £1,210

English Wrotham pottery Tyg by Henry Ifield, 12.4cm. high, 1664.
$3,300 £1,650

A rare Wrotham Tyg by George Richardson dated 1649.
$3,520 £1,760

Wrotham pottery jug by George Richardson, 6½ins. high.
$3,960 £1,980

A Wrotham slipware Tyg by George Richardson. $3,960 £1,980

ZURICH

Pair of 18th century Zurich porcelain figures representing Autumn, 8½ins. high.
$26,120 £13,060

Zurich porcelain figure representing painting, 6½ins. high.
$40,000 £20,000

19th century Canton
vase, 24ins. tall.
$110 £55

A 19th century Canton
porcelain bowl, the interior
panels of figures in landscapes
and flowers in red, blue and
yellow, 16¼ins. diam.
$160 £80

One of pair of Canton
porcelain pilgrim bottles
with double handles,
painted panels of figures,
flowers and birds, 12½ins.
high. $250 £125

Pair of 19th century
Cantonese vases,
26ins. high. $380 £190

A large 19th century
Cantonese vase.
$290 £145

Cantonese ceramic
verandah seat, 1860,
19ins. high.
$480 £240

A large early 19th
century Canton
porcelain baluster
vase, 35½ins. high.
$1,060 £530

A large 19th century Canton
circular punch bowl and
matching stand, with blue
enamelled ground strewn
with gilt meanders, foliage
and panels of figures. $1,700 £850

One of a pair of
Canton vases.
$5,500 £2,750

CH'ENG HUA

Ch'eng Hua period (1465-87) porcelain vase decorated in underglaze blue, 8.6cm.
$24,200 £12,100

Ch'eng Hua period porcelain bowl decorated in under-glaze blue, 5.6cm diam. $39,600 £19,800

Tou ts'ai wine cup decorated in blue, red, yellow and pale green, with six character mark of Ch'eng Hua. $88,000 £44,000

Ch'eng Hua stem cup decorated in iron-red and underglaze blue, with various fabulous animals, 4 ins high.
$105,600 £52,800

Chinese porcelain jar of the Ch'eng Hua period, decorated in underglaze blue, 10.3cm.
$160,000 £80,000

Blue and white porcelain saucer dish from the reign of Ch'eng Hua, 8 ins diam. $352,000 £176,000

CH'IA CH'ING

A superb Ch'ia Ch'ing fish bowl, 15½ ins high.
$4,600 £2,300

Ch'ia Ch'ing period (1522-66) double gourd vase painted in blue and red on a yellow ground, 21.6cm. $78,000 £39,000

A Ch'ia Ch'ing vase decorated with yellow dragons on a coral background, 12¼in.
$215,000 £107,500

A large blue and white Ch'ien Lung plate decorated with flowers and shrubs and rust and gilt ducks, 15¼ ins.
$44 £22

A Ch'ien Lung blue and white vase.
$170 £85

One of a pair of famille rose porcelain plates of the Ch'ien Lung period, 9 ins.
$200 £100

Ch'ien Lung period two handled censer with a frieze of the eight immortals, 11 ins wide.
$230 £115

An Oriental double gourd vase painted in the famille verte palette, of the Ch'ien Lung period, 16 ins high.
$310 £155

A rare European subject oviform tea caddy of the early Ch'ien Lung period, 3¼ ins.
$380 £190

Rare tortoise tureen of the Ch'ien Lung period. $670 £335

A large famille rose bowl with a central medallion of a European figure on foot with hounds, from the Ch'ien Lung period, 13 ins.
$790 £395

Large saucer shaped dish of the Ch'ien Lung period with famille rose and famille verte decoration, 17 ins.
$910 £455

105

One of a pair of
Ch'ien Lung
export plates
decorated with
hunting scenes.
$1,100 £550

One of a pair of
'Compagnie-des-
Indes' figures of
a water buffalo,
late Ch'ien Lung
period.$1,680 £840

A Chinese porcelain
group of the Ch'ien
Lung period,
painted in famille
rose enamels.
$3,080 £1,540

A Chinese, oval, poly-
chrome fish tank of
the late Ch'ien Lung
period, 38 ins wide.
$3,410 £1,705

Blue and white
pilgrim flask of the
Ch'ien Lung period.
$15,400 £7,700

Ch'ien Lung period (1736-
95) porcelain tureen
and cover, 36.8cm wide.
$21,000 £10,500

Chinese porcelain vase of
the Ch'ien Lung period,
decorated with coloured
enamels, 16 cm high.
$37,000 £18,500

Chinese enamelled
porcelain tureen,cover
and stand of the
Ch'ien Lung period.
$64,000 £32,000

One of a pair of
Chinese porcelain
pheasants, in famille
rose colours, of the
Ch'ien Lung period,
33 cm.
$132,000 £66,000

Baluster shaped porcelain vase decorated with famille rose enamels, Tao Kuang period, 7¼ ins. **$44 £22**

Pair of blue enamelled porcelain models of dogs, 4 ins high, Chinese 19th century. **$44 £22**

A 19th century Chinese porcelain jardiniere with blue and white prunus flower decoration, 8 ins. **$44 £22**

A 19th century copy of a Wan Li baluster vase decorated in underglaze blue. **$50 £25**

A late 18th century Chinese blue and white porcelain tankard, 5¼ ins. **$50 £25**

A Kuang Tung ware white plate banded in pale blue with a polychrome foliage pattern, 14¾ ins. **$72 £36**

Two Chinese porcelain spill vases decorated in blue with figures and landscapes, 12 ins **$80 £40**

A Chinese unglazed pottery standing figure in gathered robes wearing a dignitary's crown. **$116 £58**

Chinese crackleware vase decorated with the Imperial Dragon and peony tree. **$120 £60**

CHINESE

Early 19th century Chinese sang de boeuf vase in ovoid form. $160 £80

Heavy 19th century green ground Chinese dish with figure, bird and scenery decoration. $160 £80

One of a pair of Chinese stoneware fish tanks with dragons and scroll design, 20 ins diam., 20 ins high. $200 £100

Blue and white Chinese porcelain stem cup, transitional period, 4½ ins. $260 £130

18th century Chinese export plate, the border of an escalloped ribbon, the centre a figure group containing Britannia. $300 £150

19th century Chinese blue and white bulbous vase and cover on stand. $300 £150

Early 19th century Chinese porcelain tea caddy with English silver collar and lid, hallmarked London, 1828, maker W.B. $340 £170

One of a pair of ruby ground vases and covers of the Tao Kuang period. $410 £205

A Chinese rouleau vase, 23 ins. $500 £250

108

18th century Yuan
celadon dish. $530 £265

Chinese porcelain
orchid vase of the
Tao Kuang period.
$530 £265

Tang H'si shallow
dish, 15½ ins diam.
$620 £310

A 19th century
Chinese jardiniere,
16 ins high and
18 ins diam. $670 £335

19th century
Chinese rectan-
gular blue and
white jardin-
iere, 13 ins.
$720 £360

One of a fine pair of
19th century vases
depicting Chinese
garden scenes.
$840 £420

Pair of 19th century
export figures of an
Emperor and
Empress. $940 £470

A Chinese 'tobacco-
leaf' pattern teapot.
$940 £470

Chinese porcelain dog
made in the 18th
century, 6¼ ins high.
$1,150 £575

CHINESE

One of a pair of 19th century Chinese porcelain vases, 24 ins.
$1,250 £625

A fine and rare Chinese porcelain Imperial dragon, standing on intricately carved wood stand surmounting carved base, 15in. long by 8½in. wide. $1,320 £660

Mid 17th century Chinese vase.
$1,510 £755

One of a pair of Chinese garden seats.
$1,510 £755

One of a pair of 19th century Chinese tureens in the form of sleeping elephants on an ormolu base. $1,640 £820

18th century Chinese porcelain dog. $1,640 £820

Chinese porcelain cockerel circa 1800. $1,800 £900

One of a pair of Chinese armorial two-handled tureens and covers.
$1,920 £960

A very fine Shibayama vase inlaid on a gold lacquered ground.
$2,300 £1,150

110

18th century
Chinese porcelain
basket, mounted
in ormolu, 8¼ ins
high. $5,830 £2,915

One of a pair of attractive
18th century grey crack-
led glaze Kuan vases with
French ormolu mounts,
19¼ ins high. $3,300 £1,650

A Chinese oval
fish tank, 3ft.
2 ins wide.
$3,410 £1,705

Very rare Chinese
Ting Yao bottle
from the 11th
century A.D., 11¾
ins high.
$15,400 £7,700

Chinese white porcelain
ewer of the Liao
dynasty, with a
simulated cane work
handle. $12,100 £6,050

18th century Chinese
goose tureen, 12ins.
long. $15,180 £7,590

Pair of enamelled Kakiemon
tigers seated on rockwork,
25 cm high, late 17th century.
$18,000 £9,000

Sung dynasty
jar decorated
with three
stylised leaf
sprays, 5¼
ins. $25,300 £12,650

15th century Chinese
porcelain pot-pourri
vase with 18th
century French
ormolu mountings,
17¾ ins.
$34,650 £17,325

111

CHINESE

One of a pair of 18th century Chinese porcelain dancers, 17½ ins. high. $56,000 £28,000

One of a pair of 18th century Chinese porcelain monkeys, 9¼ ins high. $76,000 £38,000

14th century Chinese vase in blue and white porcelain, 14½ ins high. $90,000 £45,000

Chinese Tz'u Chou vase of the Sung dynasty painted in dark brown and with a leaf green glaze, 26 cm. $110,000 £55,000

15th century Chinese blue and white vase, 13½in. $300,000 £150,000

Chinese wine ewer made in the 14th century and painted in copper red, 12¾ ins. $350,000 £175,000

An exceptionally fine Chinese porcelain moon flask. $360,000 £180,000

Mid 14th century Chinese wine jar. $480,000 £240,000

A 14th century Mei P'ing of octagonal section, painted in blue with shaped panels of flowers. $500,000 £250,000

112

Famille rose plate, 18th century, 9 ins diam. $80 £40

An 18th century famille rose bottle vase. $100 £50

One of a pair of 18th century famille rose saucer dishes, 9 ins diam. $130 £65

One of a pair of famille rose baluster vases, 14½ ins high. $430 £215

One of a pair of famille rose vases, 17½ ins high. $530 £265

A coloured saltglaze mug decorated in famille rose style · $1,150 £575

One of a massive pair of famille rose vases, 36 ins high. $5,500 £2,750

18th century famille rose fish tank, 23ins. diam. $6,000 £3,000

An exceptionally fine famille rose stylised elephant. $29,000 £14,500

FAMILLE VERTE

A small 19th century famille verte bowl.
$24 £12

A K'ang Hsi baluster vase with cut down neck decorated in the famille verte style, 11½ ins.
$220 £110

Famille verte rect-angular teapot and cover with simu-lated bamboo handle, (knob restored). $340 £170

A famille verte tea caddy.
$470 £235

A fine pair of K'ang Hsi famille verte porcelain bottles.
$530 £265

A famille verte deep circular dish of the K'ang Hsi period, decorated with floral designs, 14½ ins diam.
$1,780 £890

HAN

Chinese green glazed pottery dog of the Han dynasty, 13½ ins long. $5,280 £2,640

Chinese Han dynasty figure of a Court attendant, with detachable head, 68.6cm. high, (206BC - AD220).
$26,000 £13,000

Grey pottery ram's head of the Han dynasty.
$115,500 £57,750

19th century
shaped Imari
dish 9½ ins
wide. $24 £12

A 19th century Imari
china bowl, 9 ins diam.
$40 £20

A 20th century Imari
plate decorated with
six panels of birds
and flowers in poly-
chrome, 12½in.
diam. $44 £22

An Imari circular box
and lid decorated in
underglaze blue with
panels of rust and
green chrysanthemums.
              $70 £35

One of a pair of
Imari vases,
15 ins tall. $72 £36

One of a set of
seven 19th
century Imari
shell dishes.
      $110 £55

19th century Japanese
Imari ovoid jar and
cover, 7 ins high. $120 £60

A 19th century
Japanese Imari
dish, 11½ ins
diam. $120 £60

A 19th century
Japanese Imari
jardiniere,
13 ins diam.
      $160 £80

One of a pair of 19th century Japanese Imari baluster vases, 12in. high. $190 £95

Large 19th century Imari vase and cover, 18 ins high. $200 £100

One of a pair of 19th century Japanese Imari baluster vases, 12½ ins high. $200 £100

One of a pair of finely decorated 19th century Imari vases, 15 ins. $320 £160

Pair of Imari dishes, 25in. diam. $470 £235

17th century Japanese Arita vase. $860 £430

Imari temple vase in multi-colour with cartouches of prunus blossoms and kiri flowers, signed Fukushina. $900 £450

Late 17th century Imari porcelain 'Barber's Bowl', 10¾in. diameter. $1,000 £500

Imari style jardiniere and stand. $1,400 £700

17th century Imari
charger, 54cm. diam.
$2,110 £1,055

Late 17th century Arita
dog decorated in black,
iron red and turquoise
green, 23cm. long.
$2,200 £1,100

One of pair of late
17th century,
Japanese Arita
vases, 46 cm. high.
$3,200 £1,600

One of a pair of
early Imari vases,
22 ins high.
$3,740 £1,870

Pair of octagonal
baluster vases and
covers, 70 cm high.
$4,400 £2,200

One of a pair of 18th
century Arita Imari
high shouldered jars, 30
in. high, with carved
wooden stands.
$6,000 £3,000

Japanese Arita porcelain
vase decorated in Ko-
Kutani style, circa 1688.
$17,320 £8,660

A pair of late
17th century
Imari jars in
Kutani porce-
lain 38.8 cm.
$18,700 £9,350

Japanese 17th century
vase in Arita porcelain,
enamelled in the
Kakiemon style,
21.5 cm. $18,940 £9,470

A Japanese china baluster shaped vase decorated with a figure in famille verte colours, 18½ins. high. $30 £15

19th century Japanese red and gilt two handled porcelain pot pourri with bird and figure decoration, 7ins. tall. $30 £15

19th century Japanese china vase, 12¼ins. high. $40 £20

A Japanese dish with hexagonal lotus panelled edge, decorated with a pattern of leaves, 14½ins. diam. $116 £58

Japanese Art Nouveau Zeit Geist cloisonne vase, with damaged base, 46cm. high. $250 £125

One of a set of five Japanese earthenware tea bowls, circa 1890. $410 £205

One of a pair of 19th century Japanese double gourd vases 15¼ ins high. $570 £285

17th century Japanese Ko-Kutani porcelain dish with enamelled decoration, 36.1cm. diam. $8,800 £4,400

Late 17th century Japanese porcelain bottle, painted in Ko-Kutani style, 42cm. high. $18,400 £9,200

A large K'ang Hsi famille verte dish decorated with two figures beneath a tree, 15½ins. diam. $84 £42

K'ang Hsi period blue and white porcelain vase, 8½ins. high. $180 £90

One of a pair of K'ang Hsi period blue and white saucer dishes, 8½ins. diam. $180 £90

A famille verte perfume casket of square section, on four cabriole feet, 5ins. high, K'ang Hsi. $190 £95

Chinese teapot of the K'ang Hsi dynasty about 1680 decorated in famille verte. $380 £190

A K'ang Hsi famille verte tea caddy, 6¼ins. high. $380 £190

One of a pair of K'ang Hsi blue and white baluster vases, 13½ins. high. $530 £265

A pair of K'ang Hsi shaped enamel-sur-bisque dishes. $530 £265

19th century Chinese vase, painted in the underglaze blue and green manner of the K'ang Hsi period, 17½ins. high. $600 £300

119

A K'ang Hsi shallow dish, decorated with floral design. $670 £335

A pair of K'ang Hsi period pear shaped blue and white vases, 7½ins. high. $670 £335

Famille verte porcelain teapot of the K'ang Hsi period. $710 £355

One of a pair of blue and white dishes decorated with the eight horses of Mu Wang, K'ang Hsi period. 7¾ins. diam. $1,340 £670

A fine Chinese rouleau vase, of the K'ang Hsi period, 17¾ins. high. $1,630 £815

K'ang Hsi blue and white porcelain dish depicting the Chinese Taoist Pu-Tai. $2,640 £1,320

One of a pair of Chinese porcelain ewers and covers of the K'ang Hsi period, painted in famille verte colours, 25.5cm. high. $6,930 £3,465

K'ang Hsi period porcelain figures of Lung-Nu and Shan-Ts'ai, 55.7cm. and 44.5cm. high respectively. $8,400 £4,200

One of a pair of Game cocks in Chinese porcelain from the reign of K'ang Hsi, 10½ins. high. $105,600 £52,800

An early 15th century
Chinese Ming vase.
$4,400 £2,200

Ming dynasty jar
in blue and white
porcelain, 15th
century, 5¼ins.
diam. $8,800 £4,400

Fine mid 16th century
Ming 'Wh Ts'ai' jar,
7½ins. high.
$150,000 £75,000

NANKIN

Blue and white Nankin
tankard with delicate
geometric border around
rim, the body decorated
with a landscape scene,
circa 1790, 4½ins. high.
$90 £45

A blue and white
Nankin serving
dish and cover.
$220 £110

A very rare late 18th
century Nankin
porcelain supper set,
in blue and white,
circa 1780. $300 £150

One of a set of four
blue and white Nankin
porcelain serving dishes.
$660 £330

One of a pair of
round blue and
white Nankin
vases, 24ins. high.
$720 £360

Nankin tureen, decorated
in polychrome with
Oriental garden scenes
and with a domed cover.
$1,010 £505

SATSUMA

Satsuma saki cup, 19th century, with detailed flowers on a cream background. $14 £7

Large 19th century blue and white Satsuma ginger jar. $24 £12

One of a pair of Satsuma ware vases, decorated with landscapes, and portrait heads, 10ins. high. $36 £18

19th century Satsuma pail decorated with flowers, 12ins. high. $72 £36

19th century Satsuma jardiniere decorated with figure scenes, 27.5cm. high. $84 £42

19th century Satsuma figure of a Samurai, on a carved wooden stand. $96 £48

One of a pair of large Satsuma vases on an ebonised stand, 37ins. high. $1,060 £530

Outstanding Japanese Satsuma bowl with a gilt encrusted pictorial scene of the arrival of Chinese envoys, dated 1804. $1,200 £600

19th century Satsuma figure of a school girl, 72.5cm. high. $2,400 £1,200

122

A cream glaze pottery amphora with double dragon handles, T'ang dynasty. $1,440 £720

A T'ang amber glazed pottery figure of a Bactrian Camel, 16½ins. high. $5,720 £2,860

One of a pair of glazed pottery figures of ladies from the T'ang dynasty (618-906), 34.3 and 35.6cm. high. $20,350 £10,175

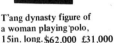

T'ang dynasty figure of a woman playing polo, 15in. long. $62,000 £31,000

T'ang dynasty ceramic figure of a horse, the body covered in a finely crackled chestnut glaze, 24in. long. $55,000 £27,500

A T'ang dynasty figure of a horse, 28ins. wide. $72,000 £36,000

YUNG CHENG

Famille rose saucer dish decorated with equestrian warriors from the Yung Cheng period. $1,100 £550

One of a pair of jars and covers of the Yung Cheng period (1723-35) enamelled with colours within ruby coloured borders, 63.5cm. high. $8,320 £4,160

One of a pair of Yung Cheng period bowls painted in the Ku Yueh-Hsuan style, (1723-35), 12.2cm. diam. $28,600 £14,300

123

INDEX

Chinese:

K'ang Hsi

Han

Mei P'ing

Sung

Ming

Satsuma

Tang

Japanese

Imari